BUILDING

AMERICA

THE
Golden Gate Bridge

Craig A. Doherty and Katherine M. Doherty

A BLACKBIRCH PRESS BOOK

WOODBRIDGE, CONNECTICUT

Special Thanks

The authors wish to thank the many librarians who helped them find the research materials for this series—especially Donna Campbell, Barbara Barbieri, Yvonne Thomas, and the librarians at the New Hampshire State Library.

Thanks also to Mary Currie—Public Information Officer for the Golden Gate Bridge, Highway and Transportation District—for all her valuable help on this project.

Published by Blackbirch Press, Inc.
260 Amity Road
Woodbridge, CT 06525

© 1995 Blackbirch Press, Inc.
First Edition

Printed in China

10 9 8 7 6 5 4

Photo Credits

Cover: ©J. Messerschmidt/Leo de Wys, Inc.
Page 4: ©Ed Caldwell/Leo de Wys, Inc.; page 6: ©Fridmar Damm/Leo de Wys, Inc.; page 8: Library of Congress; page 11: National Portrait Gallery; page 15: UPI/Bettmann: page 37: ©Rick Rusing/Leo de Wys, Inc.; page 38: ©Peter Tatinger/Leo de Wys, Inc.; page 41: ©Michael J. Howell/Leo de Wys, Inc.; pages 42–43: ©Steve Vidler/Leo de Wys, Inc. Pages 9, 16, 18, 20, 21, 22, 24–28, 30–35, 40: Golden Gate Bridge, Highway and Transportation District.

Library of Congress Cataloging-in-Publication Data

Doherty, Craig A.
   The Golden Gate Bridge / by Craig A. Doherty and Katherine M. Doherty.—1st ed.
       p. cm.—(Building America)
   Includes bibliographical references and index.
   ISBN 1-56711-106-8
   1. Golden Gate Bridge (San Francisco, Calif.)—Juvenile literature. 2. San Francisco (Calif.)—Buildings, structures, etc.—Juvenile literature.
   [1. Golden Gate Bridge (San Francisco, Calif.) 2. Bridges—Design and construction.]
   I. Doherty, Katherine M. II. Title. III.+ Series: Building America (Woodbridge, Conn.)
TG25.S225D64 1995   94-29996
624'.5'097946—dc20   CIP
                                            AC

Table of Contents

Introduction

Many people believed it was impossible. They thought no one could ever build a bridge across the Golden Gate. Not only was the water too deep, they said, the winds were too fierce. Others said the tides and the waves were too powerful and it would cost too much. If someone was foolish enough to build it, the doubters argued, an earthquake would surely send it into the bay below. However impossible it seemed at the time, the Golden Gate Bridge was built. Today it links the bustling northern California city of San Francisco to communities on the north side of the bay.

The Golden Gate is the waterway that connects the Pacific Ocean to San Francisco Bay. The huge size of the bay causes very strong tides to flow in and out. The waterway is more than a mile wide, and 382 feet deep at its deepest point. Throughout the winter months it is rocked by strong winds and waves that roll in from the Pacific. Thanks to northern California's cool nights and warm days, fog often hangs over the Golden Gate, mostly in the mornings.

Bridging the Golden Gate waterway was an amazing feat of engineering. It took 388,500 cubic yards of concrete, 117,200 tons of steel, 80,000 miles of wire, $27 million, and just over four years to build such a massive structure. In addition to the materials needed for the project, there were hundreds of workers, engineers, bankers, and politicians who helped to make the bridge a reality.

Opposite:
The south tower of the Golden Gate Bridge glows brightly in the San Francisco sun.

Spanning the Bay

Although people had talked about building a bridge across the Golden Gate for a long time, it wasn't possible at first. The technology to do it wasn't available. As engineers and designers became capable of building such a bridge, other events got in the way.

World War I (1914-1918) was the first obstacle. Large numbers of American troops were sent to Europe during this time, and the many resources being put into the war effort made building the bridge a low priority. By the time the war was over, a total of 8.4 million lives had been lost.

After the war, the United States and many other countries experienced a period of peace and prosperity known as the Roaring Twenties. Many Americans felt positive about the future. New fashions and energetic dances became popular as people enjoyed a carefree attitude about life. It was during this time that the plans for the Golden Gate Bridge were finally started.

Opposite:
The Golden Gate spans the waters that connect San Francisco Bay to the Pacific Ocean.

It would take a number of years for the actual building of the bridge to begin. If it had not been for the Great Depression in the 1930s, the bridge might never have been built. During the Depression the economy collapsed, many businesses failed, and millions of people were out of work. In the San Francisco area, over twenty-five percent of the workers were without jobs. In an effort to provide jobs, the federal, state, and local governments started many "public works projects." These were large-scale programs that built highways, dams, lakes, and bridges—among other things.

Getting Started

Although many people thought about putting a bridge across the Golden Gate in the late 1800s, Charles Crocker was the first to seriously propose doing it. In 1872, Crocker wanted to build a railroad bridge across the Golden Gate. The type of trestle bridge that would have been needed, however, would have prevented many ships from passing under. It is also unlikely that this type of bridge would have stood up to the winter storms that slam into the coast from the Pacific Ocean. In the end, Crocker's idea was considered impractical and nothing ever came of it.

About 44 years after Crocker's proposal, an article by James Wilkins in the *San Francisco Call Bulletin* on August 16, 1916, called for a bridge to be built across the Golden Gate. Wilkins was a trained engineer and understood the difficulties involved. He suggested that a suspension bridge would work. A suspension bridge supports a long span in its middle by using cables that are suspended from towers at either end. At the time, ferry boats took people north and south across the bay, though there were not that many people living north of the bay. Of those who did live there, however, many felt Wilkins's idea was a good one. After a while, the Marin County Board of Supervisors publicly stated their support for a bridge. (Marin County is just across the Golden Gate from San Francisco.) Many other individuals and organizations in the area also came out in support of the idea.

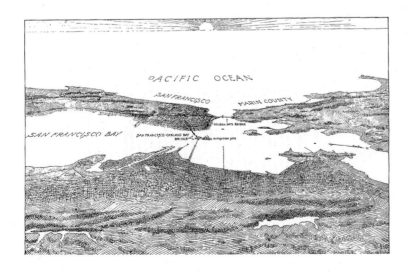

The narrow corridor that runs between the Pacific Ocean and San Francisco Bay is called the Golden Gate.

San Francisco had been the largest city in California, but the 1920 census showed that Los Angeles had surpassed it in population. In order to continue its growth, San Francisco would need bridges to connect it to areas across the bay.

Wilkins's article was read by one notable visitor to San Francisco at the time. Joseph Baerman Strauss was a bridge builder who had come to the city on business. The thought of building a bridge across the Golden Gate excited him. It excited him so much that he spent much of the next 22 years thinking about, lobbying for, designing, and building the Golden Gate Bridge. Strauss was no newcomer to bridge construction. By 1916, he had built over 400 bridges, including bridges in Asia, Africa, Russia, South America, and the United States.

Is It Possible?

In 1919, a study had been started to see if it would be possible to build a bridge across the Golden Gate. Michael O'Shaughnessy was the San Francisco city engineer at the time. He had been in charge of rebuilding the city after the devastating 1906 earthquake that destroyed much of the city, left more than 200,000 people homeless, and killed thousands. O'Shaughnessy understood the need for the city to have bridges, and he talked to many engineers about the project. Most said it couldn't be done. Others said it could be done but it would cost about $100 million to build it. Both wanting the same thing, O'Shaughnessy and Strauss got together. After the two consulted, Strauss said he could build the bridge they wanted for only $25 million.

THE GREAT DEPRESSION AND THE NEW DEAL

On October 24, 1929, the Wall Street stock market—based in New York City—"crashed," or collapsed. Because of the collapse, prices of stocks fell to their lowest levels ever. This day, which meant financial disaster for millions of people, is commonly called Black Thursday. Black Thursday also signalled the beginning of the Great Depression. During this time, over 85,000 businesses failed and one out of every four people became unemployed. Many people lost their homes and life's savings as banks and businesses all across the country failed. The few people who were able to keep their jobs earned less money. An office worker in New York who was making $45 a week before the Depression, was making $15 a week by the end of it.

Franklin Delano Roosevelt

In addition to the financial ruin of the 1930s, it was also a time of serious natural disasters. The Dust Bowl is the name given to an area that includes the Oklahoma and Texas panhandles and nearby parts of Colorado, Kansas, and New Mexico. An extended drought from 1934 to 1937 caused huge clouds of dried soil to be blown away. The dust storms sometimes buried entire houses and could often be seen hundreds of miles away. During this time, over half the population of the Dust Bowl area had to abandon their farms to move elsewhere. Many of these people moved westward to California.

In hopes of bringing an end to the Depression, the federal government started many social welfare and economic programs. Under the leadership of President Franklin D. Roosevelt, these programs were together known as the New Deal. The New Deal included various programs such as the Civilian Conservation Corps (CCC), the Works Project Administration (WPA), the Federal Housing Administration (FHA), and the National Recovery Administration (NRA). Many public projects were funded under these and other agencies. The belief was that, if people were put to work on public projects, their earnings would help boost the economy. The Golden Gate Bridge project, started in 1933, was just one of many government efforts to create jobs and stimulate the economy.

The Great Depression lasted throughout the 1930s. Many historians believe that it was the beginning of World War II in 1941 that finally stimulated the economy of the United States enough to end the Great Depression. The Golden Gate Bridge project, in part, was an effort to create jobs in the bay area.

As part of the planning stage, Strauss asked O'Shaughnessy to have the bottom of the bay surveyed. They checked the depth of the water across the channel and examined the kind of rock that would be available at the bottom. For a job such as this, Strauss would need solid bedrock on which to set the bridge's towers.

Strauss's first plan called for a bridge that was a combination of a cantilevered and a suspension bridge. A cantilevered bridge supports the roadway directly on its towers. The water depths on the north side, however, made it impossible to use the original design. The only way to bridge the channel was to use a suspension bridge.

Once O'Shaughnessy and Strauss believed they could successfully build the bridge, politics came into the picture. In 1923, the California state legislature passed a bill that allowed the establishment of a Golden Gate Bridge and Highway District. The district, which included San Francisco and the five counties on the north end of the bridge, was formed in 1928. The Bridge District's job was to oversee the project and run the bridge once it was built. Over the next few years, many people spoke up both for and against the building of the bridge.

Some people felt such a large bridge would destroy the natural beauty of the bay. The ferry company that shuttled people back and forth was afraid it would be put out of business. Some people who lived on the northern side of the channel were wary of the access people would have to their area. Farmers were afraid that all the traffic and tourists would disturb their farms. There were many people, however, who were in favor of the project. The members of the Bridging the Golden Gate Association, for example, worked hard to see the bridge actually become a reality.

The land on both ends of the bridge was owned by the U.S. military. Before any plans could move forward, the military would have to approve the project and give the Bridge District permission to use War Department land. An army colonel was appointed to hold hearings on the matter. For seven months, he listened to both sides of the argument. Finally, in 1924, the secretary of war approved the project. Another hurdle had now been overcome.

During this time, Strauss gave more thought to his design. In 1928, he competed against 11 other firms for the job of chief engineer on the project. In the end, Strauss's proposal was selected. Several of his rivals—Leon Moisseiff, Charles Derleth, and O.H. Ammann—were hired as consulting engineers. By the time the Bridge District was ready to finance the construction, the estimate for the final design was up to $27 million.

Trying to Raise Money

On November 4, 1930, voters in the Bridge District passed a bond issue for the construction money. This meant that the voters gave their local government the authority to borrow money. When the bonds were issued in 1930, a bank was needed to guarantee them. Only one bank came forward to do this. This bank wanted to attach so many requirements to the bonds that it would be impossible to meet their demands. Now, after 14 years of planning, the project was again in trouble.

Looking Back at Bridges

People have been building bridges for thousands of years. The earliest bridges were probably nothing more than a log placed over a stream. As people learned to build more sophisticated structures, bridges became larger and longer. The engineers of the Roman Empire were expert bridge builders and some of their bridges are still in use today, almost 2,000 years later! The Romans used arches to support their bridges—a design that is still popular. One of the most spectacular Roman bridges is the Alcantra Bridge over the Tagus River in Spain. The roadway is 102 feet above the water and has six 100-foot stone arches. The largest arch-span bridge in the world is the Gladesville Bridge in Sydney, Australia. It is made from reinforced concrete and spans 1,000 feet.

Truss bridges and cantilevered bridges are built directly on their supporting towers. The most spectacular and graceful bridge design is the suspension bridge. When a suspension bridge is built, heavy cables are strung over towers and anchored to the shores at either end of the bridge. The roadway is literally suspended from the cables. Using this system, great distances can be

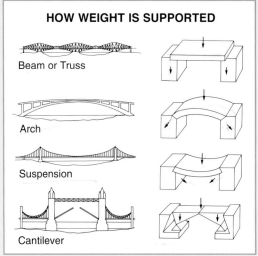

HOW WEIGHT IS SUPPORTED

Beam or Truss

Arch

Suspension

Cantilever

spanned. When it was completed, the Golden Gate Bridge had the longest bridge span in the world, a total of 4,200 feet. In 1964, the Verrazano-Narrows Bridge in New York became the world's longest with a span of 4,260 feet. The bridge that currently holds the distinction of the greatest span was completed in 1980 and crosses the Humber River in England. It has a span of 4,626 feet. Two other bridges, the Great Belt East Bridge in Denmark and the Akashi-Kaikyo Bridge in Japan, will be even longer when they are completed.

Suspension bridges across even greater distances may be built in the future. Engineers believe they will be able to span exceptionally long distances when they have perfected the use of composite materials presently used in building fighter jets and space shuttles. Materials such as graphite and kevlar are much stronger and much lighter than steel. When these materials are ready for structural use, builders might be able to bridge the English Channel between Britain and France, or even the Straits of Gibraltar, which separates southern Spain from the African continent.

Joseph Strauss was a willful and determined man, and he was not going to lose his greatest challenge without a fight. In order to raise money for construction, he took it upon himself to go see A.P. Gianinni, the president and founder of the Bank of America. After listening to Strauss, Gianinni went to his board of directors and got approval to back the bonds. Yet another problem had now been solved.

Because the country was in the middle of the Depression, many people were concerned about getting Americans back to work. By 1930, one out of every four workers in the bay area was out of work. The Bridge District decided that it should employ as many local workers as possible. To be hired for the construction project, a candidate was supposed to have lived within the Bridge District for at least a year. Specialists, like engineers, divers, crane operators, ironworkers, and cable spinners, however, did not have to be from the area.

Joseph Strauss was the driving force behind the Golden Gate Bridge project.

In January 1933, with the financing in place and the design in its final stages, it was time to begin construction. On February 26, 1933, the official ground-breaking ceremony was held. So many people attended that a model of the bridge was almost crushed by the crowd. Some estimate that over 200,000 people attended the ceremony.

Laying the Foundations

The actual construction of the Golden Gate Bridge involved the creation of many different elements. First, anchorages, or special supports, needed to be built on either end of the Golden Gate. These would anchor the cables from which the bridge's roadway would be suspended. Piers, or footings, had to be constructed for the bridge's giant towers to rest on. Then the two towers had to be erected. Once the towers were in place, cables needed to be spun across the span. The roadway then had to be hung from the cables, and the approach roads needed to be built at either end of the bridge.

It has been estimated that building the Golden Gate Bridge required 25 million hours of work. If each worker's hours were totalled up, that would come to three and a quarter million days of labor!

Opposite: Building anchorages, which hold the suspension cables in place at both ends of the bridge, was part of the first phase of construction. The Marin anchorage, on the north side of the bridge is shown, **top.** The San Francisco anchorage is shown, **bottom.**

17

Pay ranged from $11 per day for highly skilled iron-workers to $5.50 per day for general laborers. Because so many people were unemployed during the Depression, competition for jobs was fierce. One way that the contractors on the job were able to keep costs down was by taking full advantage of the labor situation. Workers were hired and fired regularly. If work stopped because of a problem, the workers would be sent home without pay. If someone didn't work hard enough, they were let go. Most laborers were fortunate if they got to work half of any week.

Starting with Anchorages

The first major task in creating the bridge was building the anchorages. The anchorages are the massive concrete structures to which the suspension cables on either end of the bridge are tied. The anchorages on the San Francisco end, however, created a unique problem. The way it was planned, the bridge would go over historic Fort Point. A special arch bridge was built over the fort, and then connected to where the suspension bridge began. There were two anchorages on each end. Each anchorage started as two pits, each 80 feet deep. The pits were dug down into the bedrock to give them a solid base to which they could be attached.

To create the anchorages, wooden forms were filled with concrete. So much

Construction on the San Francisco end was complicated by the fact that historic Fort Point was located directly under the planned structure.

concrete was needed that a cement plant was built 25 miles down the California coast. At the cement plant, oyster shells were ground into a fine powder that was then turned into cement. The cement was brought to the bridge site by boat. Two mixing plants were built, one on either side of the bay. Here, the cement was mixed with gravel and water —to make concrete—and put into cement trucks. The Golden Gate Bridge was the first construction project to use mixer trucks. These trucks had large rotating drums that turned continuously to mix the concrete.

Concrete was poured into the anchorage pits through a large funnel that cement workers called the "elephant's trunk." When the concrete came out of the funnel, men in rubber boots used a special vibrating machine to pack it down and spread it evenly. As soon as the concrete had hardened, the forms were moved up and another layer of concrete was added. Soon, each huge hole was filled with a massive concrete anchor. At the top of the anchorages, eyebars stuck out. The eyebars were long steel shafts with a loop at the top. The suspension cables were to be attached to the eyebars. Before the cable could be spun, however, the towers had to be erected. And, before the towers could be built, the piers that would support them needed to be constructed.

The Challenge of the Piers

Building the piers—which were started in 1933—was the most difficult part of the job. Compared to the piers for the south tower, the north pier was not too difficult. The north pier was at least close to shore. This meant that a cofferdam could be easily built. A

A cofferdam was needed for pier construction on the Marin side of the bay.

cofferdam is a dam that keeps out water while a hole is dug for a pier. The piers needed to rest on solid bedrock and were built up using the same procedure used for the anchorages. Layer after layer of concrete and steel reinforcing were added. When the pier reached the right height, it had to be leveled. A crew with a large grinder attached to a steel boom then smoothed the surface of the pier. Any irregularity in the form greater than 1/32nd of an inch had to be ground down. When the top of the pier was smooth, huge steel plates were attached to it. The steel plates were attached with thick pins that measured six-and-a-half inches in diameter.

The major obstacle presented by the south pier was the fact that it needed to be 1,125 feet from shore in water that was over 60 feet deep. To make matters worse, the seas were too rough to permit crews to work from boats. Strauss and one of his engineers, Clifford Paine, made two decisions. First, they decided to build a fender-ring, or enclosed cofferdam, around the site of the pier. Second, they would build a trestle, or supported road, out to the site of the pier.

A Trestle Is Needed

Work began on the trestle in February 1933, and was finished before the end of that summer. It was strong enough to allow trucks and other heavy equipment to drive out to the pier site. Electricity, water pipes, and air hoses were also all run out along the structure. Building the trestle was not without its own problems. Early in the morning of August 14, 1933, the freighter *Sidney M. Hauptman* went off course in the fog and crashed into the trestle. The ship knocked away 100 feet of construction. The trestle was repaired only to be destroyed by storms in the fall of 1933. At that point, it was decided that the trestle needed to be rebuilt to be made stronger.

A fender-ring enclosed the site for the San Francisco pier before construction. The trestle, which led out to the fender-ring, enabled trucks and other heavy equipment to drive out to the site of pier.

While the trestle was being built, excavation was going on at the pier site. Underwater holes were drilled into the bedrock from a barge. Workers would then position blasting charges into those holes. Divers working at the site found the currents so strong that they could only work for about 10 to 15 minutes on either side of the low tide. Their diving equipment consisted only of a large, round steel helmet with a small window to look out of. They also wore rubberized canvas suits. Lead weights were attached to a diver's belt and he wore weighted shoes to keep him upright and on the bottom. An air hose was attached to the helmet and air was pumped down from the surface. Divers were also secured with a rope on the barge that lowered them slowly. The rope was also used to pull them back up. It was important to bring the divers up slowly so that their bodies could adjust to the changes in pressure.

If a diver came up too fast, he might experience an extremely painful and possibly fatal condition known as "the bends." This is when nitrogen gas bubbles in the blood escape into the joints and cause serious pain. Treatment for the bends requires a pressurized chamber for the diver that slowly reduces the atmospheric pressure

Engineers and workers could stand inside the fender-ring after it was pumped out and reinforced with concrete.

over a period of time. A decompression chamber was always at the ready on the south shore of the bay for a diver who came up too fast.

After blasting the rock on the bottom, a special clamshell power shovel was used to remove the debris and muck that was created. The strong current and the powerful waves often made it extremely difficult for the shovel operator to see what the clamshell bucket was doing below the water's surface. Almost as hard as taking material off the bottom was emptying the bucket into the barge. The action of the waves and the current would sometimes cause the bucket to swing as much as 30 feet while the operator tried to empty it into the rolling barge. It took a lot of skill and a little luck to successfully fill the barge with 500 cubic yards of material. When it was full, the barge would be hauled out to sea where it was unloaded into deep water.

When the bay bottom had been excavated and the trestle was rebuilt, it was time to build the base of the pier and put in the fender-ring. The concrete sections were 30 feet thick. During its construction, water collected in the fender-ring. When it was pumped out, workers found all sorts of interesting sea creatures trapped inside. They collected the edible fish and shellfish and took them home to eat. Once the fender-ring was completed, it was 100 feet high and enclosed an area the size of a football field. Work now could begin on the actual pier.

The building and rebuilding of the trestle had put the south pier five months behind schedule and $350,000 over budget. The greatest obstacle to building the bridge, however, had now been overcome.

The Marin tower takes shape during the early stages of construction.

The San Francisco tower, as it first began to rise.

Towers of Steel

With the north pier completed, work began on the north tower. The tons of steel needed for the towers and the roadway deck were made by Bethlehem Steel in Pennsylvania—almost 3,000 miles away. From the Bethlehem mills, the steel was shipped to Philadelphia by train. In Philadelphia it was loaded onto ships, which brought the steel to San Francisco via the Panama Canal. Once the steel reached San Francisco, it was stored at Bethlehem Steel's yard in nearby Alameda. From there, it was easily transported to the bridge site by barge as it was needed.

There are actually five different types of steel in the Golden Gate Bridge. Different types of steel were used for different parts of the job. For example, the towers are not solid steel. They are like a beehive made with steel cells. Each cell is 42 inches square. The cells vary in length from 22 1/2 feet to 45 feet long. There are over 100 cells at the base of each tower leg. The tower legs taper to 23 cells at the top. The two legs of the towers are connected by six cross-braces.

Lifting the steel for the towers into place was a difficult problem. It was solved by building a special crane platform that had two cranes on it. Each crane was able to lift up to 85 tons. The unique aspect of the platform was that it could climb the tower legs as they were built. The platform's legs attached to both columns. The legs could be released and the cranes would lift the platform up higher on the tower. As the towers got higher, an elevator was installed for the workers. Because it could only carry

SAFETY FIRST

At the time the Golden Gate Bridge was built, it was assumed that one person would die for every million dollars spent on major construction projects. Joseph Strauss and the other engineers thought this estimate was unreasonable. Because of his special dedication to keeping his workers healthy, safety was stressed in all aspects of the job. A number of new safety procedures were first introduced during the Golden Gate project. The bridge was one of the first major constructions where workers were required to wear safety helmets. In addition to the leather helmets, special goggles were developed to protect eyesight. Workers building the towers and spinning the cables often found themselves so high up that they were above the fog. Looking at the sun reflecting off the fog often caused a condition similar to snow blindness. The goggles had tinted lenses that protected the workers' eyes.

From the workers' viewpoint, the most dangerous part of building the bridge was erecting the steel for the roadway. As the engineer, Strauss knew this, too. To insure the safety of the workers, he had huge nets made, similar to those used in circuses. These hung 10 feet below the roadway and also extended out

Workers stand high above the bay.

to the sides and in front of the area being worked on. It gave the workers and their families confidence to know that, if they slipped on the narrow steel beams, they would land in a net instead of 200 feet below in the rough, cold waters of the bay. This was the first time ever a net had been used during a bridge construction project. During the construction of the roadway, 19 workers fell into the net. The men who fell into the net formed an informal club they called the "Halfway to Hell Club." Today, nets are a standard part of any bridge project.

For the first three and a half years of work, there were—amazingly—no fatal accidents. There were, however, two serious accidents during the final stages of construction. On October 21, 1936, one man was killed when a fitting on a derrick broke free. The most serious accident occurred on February 17, 1937, when the bridge was almost done. Workers were removing forms from the roadway when their scaffolding let go. Although the scaffolding and the 12-man crew ended up in the net, the weight of the 10-ton scaffolding was too much for the net to hold. The net and the scaffolding fell, and 10 of the men died. A plaque was erected to their memory near the San Francisco end of the bridge.

10 to 12 people at a time, workers would sometimes have to wait up to 20 minutes at the end of the day for their turn to ride down. Once they were finished, each of the towers stood 746 feet high, contained 22,200 tons of steel, and 600,000 rivets.

On top of each column of the tower a huge cable saddle had to be attached. This equipment would hold the three-foot-thick cable in place. The cable saddles were made of three sections of cast steel. Assembled, the saddles weighed 160 tons each. Rollers were installed in the saddles so the cables could move as they were spun in place.

Once the pier was completed for the south tower, work proceeded quickly. The crews had now gained valuable experience from working on the north tower. The slogan of the workers and their bosses was "350 a day or you're out." This meant that the riveting crews were expected to set 350 rivets a day or they would be fired. One day, as the south tower neared completion, it suddenly started to sway. Many of the workers scrambled quickly downward. The swaying became so severe that workers who stayed up top became sick. One worker was caught in the elevator as it swung back and forth on its cables. The swaying, as it turned out, was caused by an earthquake. The next day, workers again felt the swaying as an after-shock rocked the area. Though it was an extremely frightening experience, the engineers and designers were relieved to see that the tower was able to withstand an earthquake, even before the bridge was completed.

Top: *Cable saddles on top of each tower held the three-foot-thick cables in place.*
Bottom: *The cable as it enters the cable saddle.*

A RIVETING STORY

There are 1.2 million metal rivets just in the two towers of the Golden Gate Bridge. Rivets are used to fasten pieces of steel together. Each rivet is about six inches long and an inch in diameter, with a rounded head on one end. Riveting was a very important job during the construction of the bridge. It was done by teams of workers. Each team consisted of three people: a "heater," a "bucker-up," and a "riveter."

The heater worked at a small portable burner where he would heat the rivets until they were white hot. During the construction of the bridge towers, the teams were often separated by great distances. Pneumatic tubes were used to send the hot rivets from the heater to the bucker-up. A pneumatic tube is a long series of pipes attached to an air pump. The pump creates suction so, when the rivets were put into the tube at one end, they would travel quickly to the other end. The bucker-up would grab the rivet with tongs and put it into the hole to be riveted. He would then use an iron bar to hold the rivet in place while the riveter hammered the other end. As the rivet cooled, it would become shorter and pull the two pieces of steel tightly together.

Each tower contains more than 600,000 rivets.

The towers of the bridge were built with steel tubes that were about 42 inches square and ranged in height from 22 1/2 to 45 feet tall. Riveting inside the tubes was very difficult. At first, many of the riveting crews became sick. It turned out that the steel had been treated with a lead paint. The hot rivets caused the lead around the holes to be released in the smoke and fumes. Many of the team members were suffering from lead poisoning. As a result, respirators were provided for the men and an effort was made to better ventilate the tubes. After the ventilation was improved, everyone recovered and no further lead poisoning problems arose. The engineers also had the steel company in Pennsylvania use lead-free paint on any new tubes.

Once they had completed work on the towers, the riveting crews were glad to begin work on the roadway. On the roadway they were out in the open air and the pneumatic tubes were replaced with "catchers." The heater would actually throw the hot rivets to the catcher. The catcher would then catch a hot rivet in a wire basket. At that point, the bucker-up would remove the rivet from the basket with tongs and place it in the hole.

3

The Final Elements

Once the foundation structures of the bridge were complete, it was time to begin work on the two final major elements: the cables and the roadway. Although completing this work was by no means easy, it was relatively simple and straightforward compared to the complications of the piers and towers.

Spinning the Cables

The first task at this stage was to assemble the bridge's massive cables. On smaller bridges, cables are spun on the ground and then hoisted into place. The cables for this bridge, however, would weigh over 12,000 tons each. There was no way something of that weight could be lifted over 700 feet in the air! The cables would have to be spun in place.

29

*Below: Before spinning the cable, large wire ropes were stretched from one shore to the other to be used as catwalks. **Bottom:** Four strands of cable are shown in spinning position.*

Strauss and the other engineers decided that only one company was right for the cabling job. They selected John A. Roebling & Sons of New Jersey to spin the cables. They had done the Brooklyn Bridge and were considered the most experienced cablers in the country. Their job would earn them $6 million.

On August 2, 1935, the Coast Guard closed the Golden Gate waterway to shipping. When the Golden Gate was closed, large wire ropes were strung from one shore to the other. The wire ropes were attached to the anchorages and then hoisted up to the tower tops. These wires would be used to build temporary catwalks across the bridge. The catwalks would be set three feet below

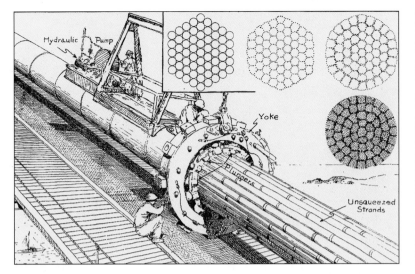

the level of the cable. From the catwalks, the workers would be able to spin the cable.

The actual cable for the Golden Gate Bridge is made up of wire that is only 0.196 inches in diameter. But there are 27,572 individual wires in each cable. By the time the cables reached their finished size, more than 80,000 miles of wire had been used. After a certain number of wires had been spun together they would be bound together into a strand. Each strand was made up of 256 wires to 462 wires.

As the job of spinning the cables progressed, the crews at the anchorages would adjust the strands and attach them to the eyebolts. Wires were adjusted at night. The cool temperatures caused the wire to contract slightly and made the adjustments more exact. When the 61 strands that make up each cable were completed, they needed to be compressed. A circular jack was used to compress the cables. The jack could apply over 4,000 pounds of force on the cable. Once the cable was compacted, special machines wrapped a layer

of fine wire around the entire cable. The finished cables measured 36 3/8 inches in diameter.

At this point, all that was left to do was attach the suspenders. Cast-steel clamps were attached to the cable every 50 feet. These served two purposes: First, they clamped the cable together. Second, they were used as saddles for the road-way suspender cables. The cable spinners finished their part of the project on May 20, 1936. It had taken them just over six months.

Every 50 feet, the finished cable was attached to the roadway for support.

Finally, the Roadway

The final construction phase was the building of the roadway, which started late in the summer of 1936. The roadway was designed to hang from the main cables, with a steel supporting frame under the surface of the road. The steel frame had to be erected first. The hardest part of erecting the steel for the roadway was keeping the weight on the cables even. Three-inch-thick wire suspender cables were hung every 50 feet along the main cable. The steel frame would be attached to the suspenders.

To keep the weight evenly distributed, the steelwork had to start at the two towers. From the towers, the crews had to work toward the middle of the bridge and to the shores at the same time. During this process, it was very important to keep the load on the cables even. If one crew slowed down for any reason, they would have to signal the other three crews to do the same.

Opposite: The first stage of roadway construction was complete when the steel supporting structure was finished.

To get the steel up to the roadway, large cranes on barges were tied to the tower footings. The steel was then brought out to the cranes by boat. The cranes lifted the steel up to the roadway and, at the roadway level, smaller cranes were set on tracks. These cranes lifted the steel and moved it out to the end of the roadway. Workers, called "connectors," guided the steel into position before the riveting teams fastened it in place.

Once the roadway was started, people in the area got more excited about the project. The local papers regularly reported on the progress of the roadway and the San Francisco community waited with great anticipation for access to the north to open up for them.

The section of roadway shown in the fore-ground is ready to receive its concrete top layer.

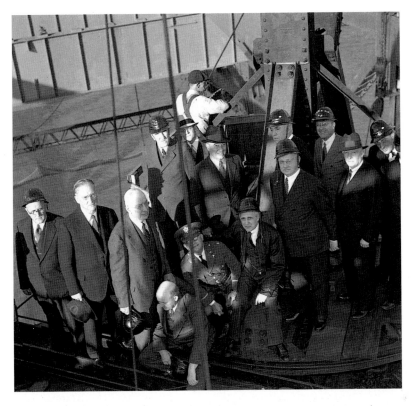

Engineers and local administrators from both sides of the bay gathered on November 18, 1936, to witness the meeting in the middle of spans from both ends of the bridge.

By November, the side spans were connected to land. On November 18, 1936, a special ceremony was held on the bridge. Representatives from both sides of the Golden Gate came out onto the bridge. They watched as Strauss took control of a crane and lowered a 100-foot section of steel into place. With that section of steel in place, the two sides of the bridge were connected. When the final elements of steelwork for the roadway were completed, it was time to pour the concrete roadbed.

The concrete was poured in three, twenty-foot-wide sections, with the two outer sections poured first. It was done this way so that a locomotive and a concrete car could travel back and forth with the concrete for the rest of the roadbed. Carpenters built wooden forms to hold the concrete. Welders put in reinforced steel bars that would be buried in the concrete. These "re-bars" added strength to the concrete.

Every 50 feet, copper and steel expansion joints were inserted in the roadbed. The expansion joints allowed the steel underneath to expand and contract without cracking the concrete. As with the steelwork, the weight of the concrete had to be added to the bridge evenly. The crews once again started working at the two towers at the same time and went in four directions at the same time.

When the two outside sections were completed, the crews turned their attention to the last section. The tracks for the cement train were pulled up as the work progressed. By the beginning of 1937, the work on the roadway was nearing completion. While the crews were building the roadway on the bridge, the approach roads were built. The hills on the north side made those approach roads especially costly and hard to build.

With the approach roads done, all that was left to do was the finish work. Railings, lights, and tollbooths now had to be installed. The railings were designed by Irving Morrow, the same architect who designed the towers. Solid railings were the standard for bridges at the time. Morrow, however, wanted motorists to be able to see the dramatic and beautiful views from the bridge so he designed his railings with slats. Special lights were used to illuminate the bridge and roadway as well. Morrow chose sodium-vapor lights, which gave off yellowish light that made it easier for motorists to see in the fog. The bridge also had to be painted.

A QUESTION OF COLOR

The orange glow of the bridge blends beautifully with its surroundings.

Painting the Golden Gate Bridge was extremely important. If left unprotected, the steel would soon rust and severely weaken the bridge. Which color to paint the structure caused much debate. Some people wanted it painted gold to match its name. Others wanted it painted grey, silver, or black—these were considered the traditional colors for a bridge.

Irving Morrow, the staff architect in Strauss's office, conducted a series of paint tests. Samples were painted onto steel panels and set out in the weather at Fort Point. Morrow checked the samples regularly and recorded the results. After some time, his recommendation was for a paint called Dulux International Orange.

This paint had stood up well in the tests, but also had other benefits. It would be easy to see by people on ships, and it also blended in with the colors of the Golden Gate area. In addition, it matched the red in the hills of Marin County. On October 6, 1936, the engineering board accepted Morrow's recommendation, and the Golden Gate Bridge has been international orange ever since.

The initial painting of the bridge was done by painters with brushes. The first paint job used over 10,000 gallons of paint and started before work on the bridge was completed. Painters had to work fast in order to protect the steel from the salt air of the bay area.

4

Opening the Bridge

On April 28, 1937, there was a special ceremony to celebrate the completion of the bridge's steelwork. For the festivities, a golden rivet was donated for use in the bridge. With Strauss and a number of dignitaries present, a riveter nicknamed Iron Horse and his bucker-up tried to install the golden rivet. Gold does not react like steel, however, and the two men struggled to set the rivet. After the ceremony ended, the two men fixed a steel rivet in place instead.

The bridge was finally completed on May 26, 1937. The next day, it was officially opened and Pedestrians Day was declared. During the first 12 hours that the bridge was open, over 200,000 people paid five cents each way to walk across the Golden Gate Bridge. The next day, the bridge was officially

Opposite:
A breath-taking aerial view of the roadway from the top of the Marin tower.

39

opened to motor vehicles. All sorts of festivities were organized to continue the celebration. On the north side, giant redwood logs blocked access to the roadway as a log-sawing contest was held to honor the opening of the bridge. People came from as far away as Alaska and Canada to witness the special events. A total of 32,300 cars crossed the bridge just on the first day! Each car paid a 50-cent toll for the car, the driver, and up to three passengers. Extra passengers had to pay 5 cents.

Strauss had completed the bridge only five months over the original promised date, and there was $1.3 million left over in the budget from the bonds that were sold. For its work, Strauss's company was given a $1 million fee. He was also given a lifetime pass to use the bridge for free. He did not use the pass for long, however—he died within just a year of the completion of the bridge.

On opening day in 1937, more than 200,000 pedestrians walked across the Golden Gate.

The Bridge Today

Since it opened in 1937, the Golden Gate Bridge has been forced to close only three times. It was first closed in 1951 because of dangerously high winds. (By 1954 bracing was added to the steel that supports the roadway.) The bridge was again closed in 1981 and 1982 because of high winds. The concern was mostly for the cars. Up that high, they could easily be blown out of their lanes.

In 1985, the bridge's roadbed was replaced at a cost of $60 million. The concrete was torn out and replaced with much lighter steel panels. By doing this, the weight of the bridge was greatly reduced

by 12,300 tons. Today, the bridge is going through a new series of renovations and strengthening measures. The engineers involved want to improve the bridge's ability to withstand a major earthquake. They also want to insure that the structure will last long into the future. Current work on the Golden Gate will cost an estimated $147 million.

As costs of repairing and maintaining the bridge have gone up, so have the tolls for cars. The original toll of 50 cents each way was reduced a number of times until it was 25 cents in 1955. Since then, it has climbed steadily. In 1971, the toll was increased to one dollar. It hit two dollars in 1981, and three dollars in 1991. In 1993, roughly 40.5 million vehicles crossed the Golden Gate Bridge.

Although there are now taller and longer bridges in the world, there are few other bridges that are recognized as easily as the Golden Gate. The bridge that people said was impossible to build has become a shining example of human engineering. It is also a permanent monument to the skill and dedication of the many people who made Strauss's dream a reality.

The Golden Gate offers a dramatic view when it is lighted at night.

Today, the Golden Gate Bridge stands as one of America's most majestic and beloved landmarks.

GLOSSARY

anchorage The massive concrete structure to which the main suspension cables are attached.

bedrock The solid rock of the earth's upper crust. It is often covered by loose sediment.

bends A dangerous condition suffered by divers who come to the surface too fast.

bonds A way of financing large public projects. Investors buy the bonds with the promise that they will be paid back plus receive interest.

bucker-up The person in a riveting crew who inserts the rivet into the steel and then holds the end securely in place while the riveter hammers down the other end.

cable saddle The cast steel top to each tower leg over which the cable passes.

cantilevered bridge A bridge that rests directly on its supporting columns.

catcher The person who catches white hot rivets in a wire basket.

catwalk A narrow walkway usually suspended in the air.

cement The ingredient in concrete—made from different things—that binds it together.

clamshell bucket A device on the end of a crane that opens and closes like a clam and is used to remove dirt and other material from a hole.

cofferdam A watertight dam that encloses a construction site that will be below the level of the surrounding water.

concrete A mixture of cement, gravel, and water that can be poured into forms. It hardens to become rock-like.

connectors The workers who are responsible for guiding the steel beams and plates into place as the crane lowers them.

crane A piece of construction equipment with a long boom that can lift heavy objects using a complex system of pulleys and cables.

cubic yard A measurement used with materials such as cement or gravel. It is equivalent to the amount of material it would take to fill a box that is three feet wide, deep, and tall.

decompression chamber A device used to treat divers who have come to the surface too fast.

engineer A person with a college degree, who oversees a wide variety of building processes. Civil and structural engineers are the people primarily involved in the building of bridges.

expansion joint A space that is left in concrete that allows for the expansion and contraction of a structure as a whole. The space is often filled with a material that will expand and contract with the main structure. The expansion joints on the Golden Gate Bridge were filled with copper and steel.

eyebar Large steel bar with loops in the end. The cables for the Golden Gate Bridge were attached to eyebars set in the concrete of the anchorages.

fender-ring A dam built to protect workers building a pier from rough seas.

graphite A black carbon material that can be formed into a fiber that is very strong.

heater The worker who heats rivets until they are white hot so that they can be used to attach two pieces of steel together.

jackhammer A tool, usually powered by air, that hits an object with great force.

kevlar A light-weight, space-age material made from graphite fibers that is stronger than steel. It is used in jet planes, space shuttles, and bulletproof vests. Someday engineers hope it can be adapted for structural use.

peen To flatten an object by hammering on it.

pneumatic tube A series of pipes and flexible tubes attached to an air pump. Objects are moved from one location to another via the tubes by the vacuum created by the pumps.

re-bar A steel reinforcing bar that is laid into a form before the concrete is poured. The re-bar makes the concrete extremely strong.

rivet A steel rod with a head on one end used to attach two pieces of steel together. The rivets are inserted into predrilled holes in the steel while they are white hot. The riveter peens down the end of the rivet, and as it cools the steel in the rivet contracts and draws the two pieces of steel tightly together.

riveter The worker who uses a jackhammer to peen down the end of the hot rivet.

scaffolding A series of temporary platforms, usually high up in the air, that workers can stand on to do their work.

suspender cable The wire cable that the roadway of a suspension bridge hangs from.

suspension bridge A bridge where the weight of the roadway is suspended from an overhead cable.

tongs Long-handled pliers that are used to pick up white hot rivets.

trestle A braced frame used to support a bridge.

trestle bridge A bridge built over a series of braced frames.

CHRONOLOGY

1872 Charles Crocker proposes building a bridge across the Golden Gate.

1906 San Francisco earthquake.

1914-1919 World War I.

1916 James Wilkins's article proposing bridging the Golden Gate is published.

1919 Study of building the bridge begins.

1921 Joseph Strauss gives city officials his original bridge design.

1923 California legislature approves the creation of the Golden Gate Bridge and Highway District.

1924 U.S. secretary of war approves bridge proposal.

1928 Golden Gate Bridge and Highway District is created.

1929 Joseph Strauss is selected as chief engineer.

1929 October 29th—Stock market crashes.

1930 Bond issue to raise money to build bridge passes.

1933 Bridge construction begins.

1933 August 14th—Freighter *Sidney M. Hauptman* hits the construction trestle.

1935 August 2nd—Golden Gate channel closes to shipping to allow wires to be attached to the anchorages and hoisted to the tower tops.

1936 Cable spinning is finished, and the roadway is started.

1936 October 21st—First person is killed during construction.

1936 November 18—Celebration is held when Joseph Strauss takes control of a crane and lowers a 100-foot-length of steel in place to connect the north and south ends of the roadway.

1937 February 17th—Ten workers die when the scaffolding they are on lets go.

1937 April 28th—Golden rivet celebration is held to mark the placing of the last rivet in the Golden Gate Bridge.

1937 May 27th Pedestrians Day is declared and 200,000 people walk across the bridge.

1937 May 28th—First vehicles cross the bridge and it is officially open to the public.

1954 Bracing is added below roadway to stiffen the bridge.

1983 Roadbed is replaced.

FURTHER READING

Ardley, Neil. *Bridges*. Ada, OK: Garrett Educational Corp., 1990.

Carlisle, Norman and Madeline. *Bridges*. Chicago: Childrens Press, 1983.

Fitzgerald, Jean. *Golden Gate Bridge*. Mahwah, NJ: Troll, 1978.

Gross, Sukey S. *Golden Gate*. Lakewood, NJ: CIS Communications, 1989.

Pelta, Kathy. *Bridging the Golden Gate*. Minneapolis, MN: Lerner, 1987.

Spangenburg, Ray, and Moser, Diane. *The Story of America's Bridges*. New York: Facts On File, 1991.

Source Notes

Boyer, David S. "Golden Gate: Of City, Ships, and Surf." *National Geographic*, July 1979, 98-104.

Brown, Allen. *Golden Gate: Biography of a Bridge*. Garden City, NY: Doubleday, 1965.

Castro, Janice. "The Benefits of Being Prepared." *Time*, October 30, 1988, 42-43.

Dillon, Richard. "Spanning the Golden Gate." *American History Illustrated*, 1987, v 22, no 3, 34-45.

Fincher, Jack. "The 'Impossible' Bridge that Spans the Golden Gate." *Smithsonian*, 1982, v 13, no 4, 98-104, 106-7.

The Golden Gate Bridge: Report of the Chief Engineer to the Board of Directors of the Golden Gate Bridge and Highway District. San Francisco, CA: Golden Gate Bridge and Highway District, 1938.

"Golden Gate Bridge Roadway Replacement." *Public Works*. April 1985, v 116, 75-77.

Ketchum, Mark A. "Probing the Golden Gate." *Civil Engineering*, v 61, no 6, July 1991, 42-45.

McGinty, Brian. "Span of Gold." *American West*, 1987, v 24, no 2, 26-34.

Pelta, Kathy. *Bridging the Golden Gate*. Minneapolis, MN: Lerner, 1987.

Pierson, John. "Famous Bridge Gets Discrete Support." *Wall Street Journal*, March 10, 1993.

Riesenberg, Felix. *Golden Gate: The Story of San Francisco Harbor*. New York: Knopf, 1940.

Trippett, Frank. "First the Shaking. Then the Flames." *Time*, October 30, 1989, 50-51.

Van der Zee, John. *The Gate: The True Story of the Design and Construction of the Golden Gate Bridge*. New York: Simon and Schuster, 1986.

Index